THE AMAZING
ANIMAL ATLAS

Dr Nick Crumpton & Gaia Bordicchia

FLYING EYE BOOKS

London | New York

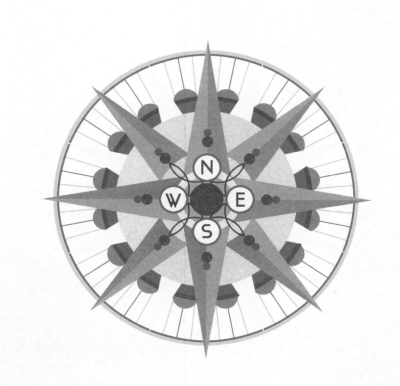

TABLE OF CONTENTS

THE TREE OF LIFE

Our planet teems with life. There could be anywhere between five million to one hundred million species on Earth! So how can we keep track of them all? We could make an enormous list, but an easier way is to think about how animals are related to each other. Here are some of the many branches that make up the tree of life.

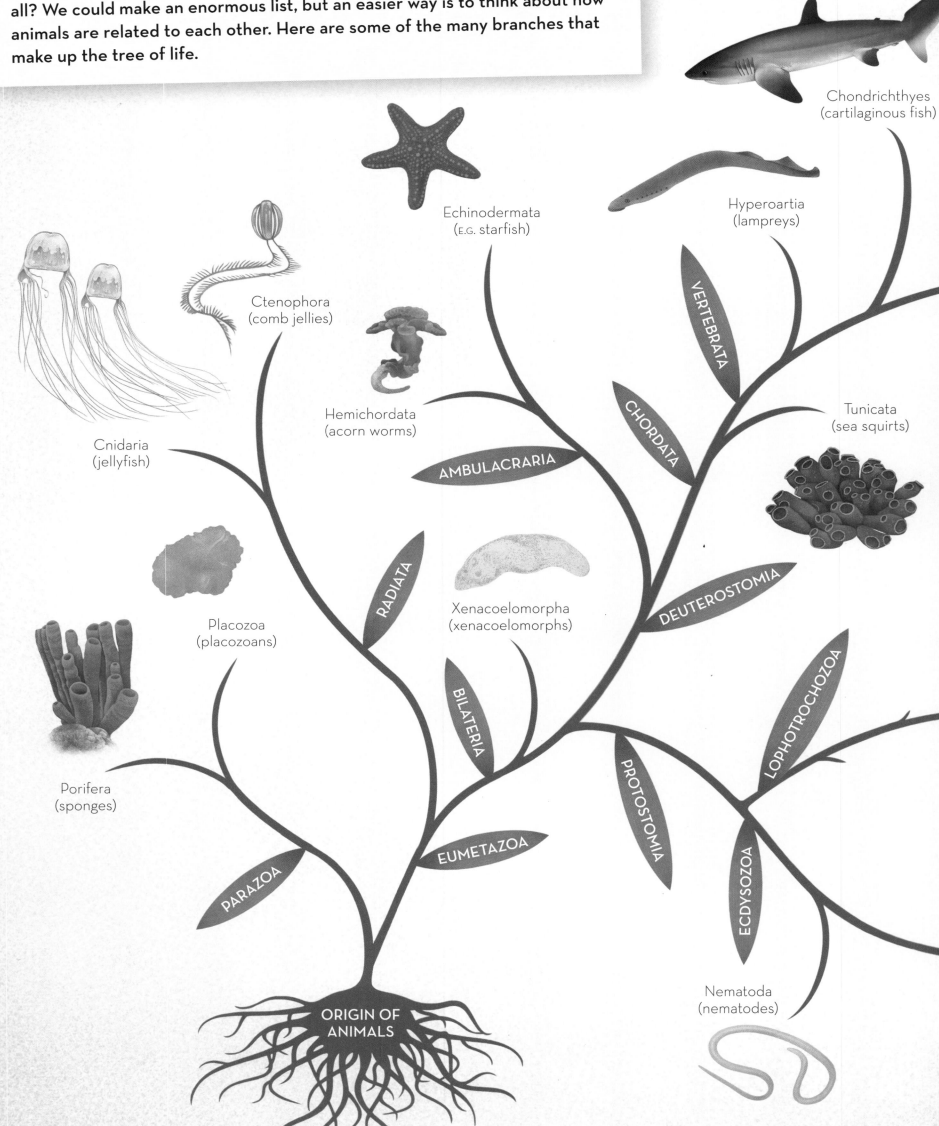

Chondrichthyes
(cartilaginous fish)

Hyperoartia
(lampreys)

Echinodermata
(E.G. starfish)

VERTEBRATA

Ctenophora
(comb jellies)

Tunicata
(sea squirts)

CHORDATA

Hemichordata
(acorn worms)

AMBULACRARIA

Cnidaria
(jellyfish)

DEUTEROSTOMIA

RADIATA

Xenacoelomorpha
(xenacoelomorphs)

Placozoa
(placozoans)

LOPHOTROCHOZOA

BILATERIA

Porifera
(sponges)

PROTOSTOMIA

PARAZOA

EUMETAZOA

ECDYSOZOA

Nematoda
(nematodes)

ORIGIN OF
ANIMALS

Osteichthyes
(bony fish)

Sarcopterygii
(lobe-finned fish)

TETRAPODA

Testudines
(E.G. turtles)

Squamata
(lizards and snakes)

Crocodilia
(crocodiles and alligators)

AMNIOTA

MAMMALIA

Amphibia
(amphibians)

Monotremata
(E.G. platypus
and echidnas)

Aves
(birds)

Laurasiatheria
(E.G. lions, bats
and whales)

Afrotheria
(E.G. moles and elephants)

Marsupialia
(E.G. tree-kangaroos
and wombats)

PLACENTALIA

Euarchontoglires
(E.G. lemurs and apes)

Xenarthra
(E.G. armadillos
and sloths)

Bivalvia
(bivalves)

Platyhelminthes
(flatworms)

Brachiopoda
(lamp shells)

Cephalopoda
(octopus and squid)

Gastropoda
(E.G. snails and
sea slugs)

MOLLUSCA

Entognatha
(springtails)

Tardigrada
(water bears)

Annelida
(annelids)

Myriapoda
(millipedes and
centipedes)

HEXAPODA

ARTHROPODA

Onychophora
(velvet worms)

Chelicerata
(scorpions and
spiders)

Crustacea
(crustaceans)

Insecta
(insects)

9

ANIMAL WORLDS

Animals all interact with each other and their environment in some way. These interactions are like a web of living things linking everything together. Biologists call this interweaving web – together with the environment the animals live in – an ecosystem.

The natural home of an animal or plant is called a habitat. Animals look and behave very differently to one another because they have evolved to live in different habitats.

DECIDUOUS WOODLANDS

These woodlands are only found between 40 and 60 degrees north or south of the equator and each season of the year is very distinct. When the leaves fall off the trees in autumn, thousands of insects use them as food and eventually break them down into soils.

RAINFORESTS

The high temperatures and rainy conditions mean that rainforests grow to be very tall and dense, supporting tens of thousands of species. The Amazon rainforest contains one in ten of all the known species on Earth!

MARINE

Marine habitats include reefs, estuaries, the abyss of the deep ocean, and the seabed itself. They make up 71 per cent of the planet's surface, but the majority of this remains completely unexplored.

MOUNTAINS

Mountains are formed when the Earth's tectonic plates crash into each other. They are cold, steep and in a state of gradual change as the plates keep moving. With steady footing and an ability to adapt to changing elevations, some animals thrive here.

POLAR REGIONS AND TUNDRA

Polar regions and tundra are at the ends of the Earth – the extreme north and south. Tundra is too cold for many plants to survive, except for moss and lichen, which take many years to grow.

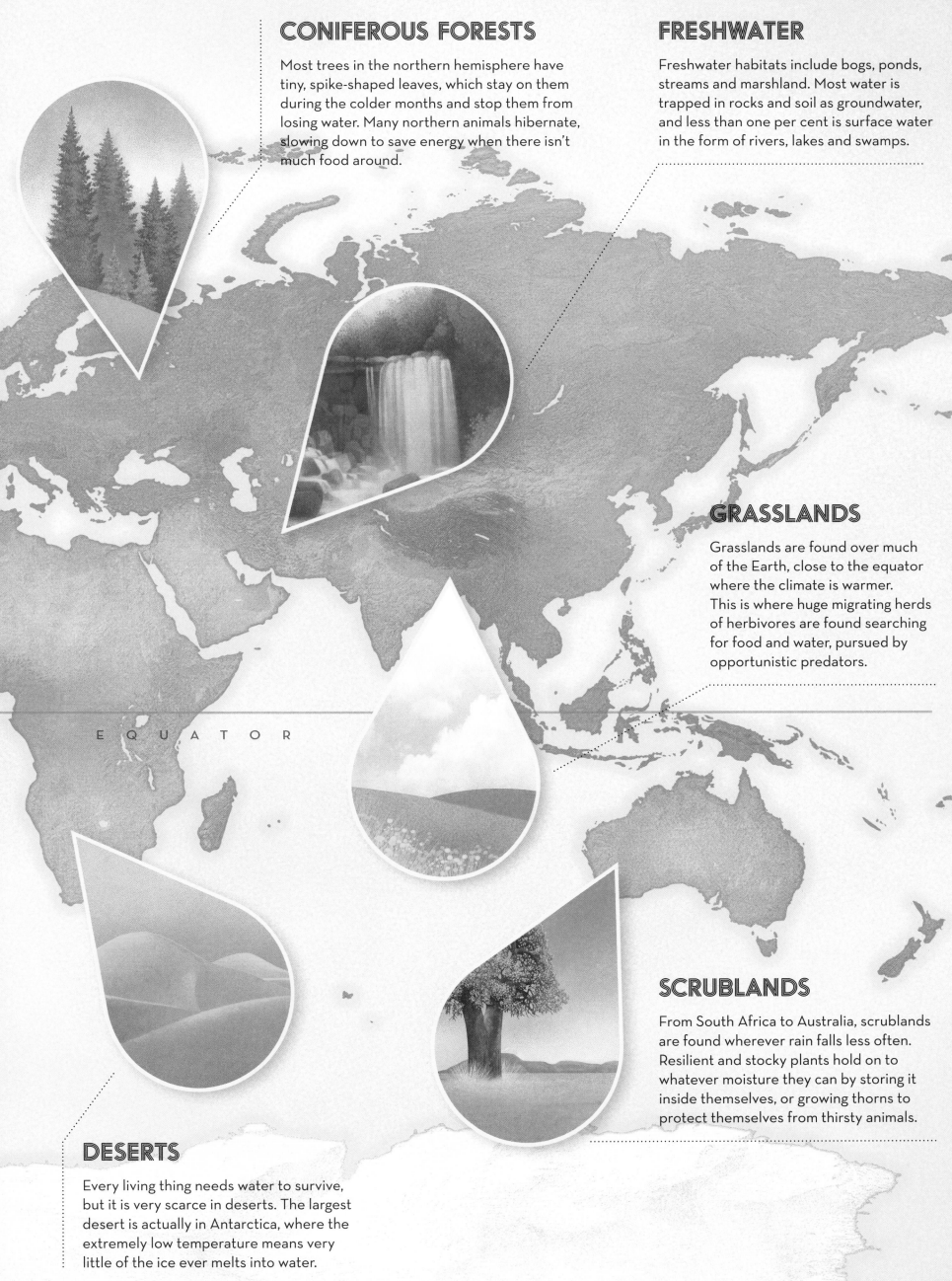

CONIFEROUS FORESTS

Most trees in the northern hemisphere have tiny, spike-shaped leaves, which stay on them during the colder months and stop them from losing water. Many northern animals hibernate, slowing down to save energy when there isn't much food around.

FRESHWATER

Freshwater habitats include bogs, ponds, streams and marshland. Most water is trapped in rocks and soil as groundwater, and less than one per cent is surface water in the form of rivers, lakes and swamps.

GRASSLANDS

Grasslands are found over much of the Earth, close to the equator where the climate is warmer. This is where huge migrating herds of herbivores are found searching for food and water, pursued by opportunistic predators.

EQUATOR

SCRUBLANDS

From South Africa to Australia, scrublands are found wherever rain falls less often. Resilient and stocky plants hold on to whatever moisture they can by storing it inside themselves, or growing thorns to protect themselves from thirsty animals.

DESERTS

Every living thing needs water to survive, but it is very scarce in deserts. The largest desert is actually in Antarctica, where the extremely low temperature means very little of the ice ever melts into water.

THE ARCTIC

The Arctic is often called the 'land of the midnight sun' because the sun never rises in the winter and never sets in the summer! Every winter the ocean freezes over, connecting the surrounding area in a massive sheet of ice, allowing animals (and people) to migrate across the North Pole.

DID YOU KNOW?

Harp seals are very fast swimmers, and can hold their breath for up to 15 minutes underwater.

SNOWY OWL
Bubo scandiacus

NARWHAL
Monodon monoceros

HARP SEAL PUP
Pagophilus groenlandicus

ARCTIC WHALES

Known as the 'unicorns of the sea', the narwhals are famous for their single swirling tusk, which is actually a tooth. Second only to the blue whale in weight, the bowhead whale has the largest mouth of any animal on the planet. Beluga whales' clicks, grunts, squeals and whistle sounds have earned them the name 'sea canary'.

BOWHEAD WHALE
Balaena mysticetus

EBONY BEARS

Covered in thick white fur for insulation, the polar bear's skin is actually black, like its nose and paws. They can sniff out prey almost a kilometre away and a metre under snow! Polar bears are solitary animals, but the mothers are famously protective of their cubs.

POLAR BEAR
Ursus maritimus

BELUGA WHALE
Delphinapterus leucas

NORTH PACIFIC OCEAN

UNITED STATES

NORTH POLE

CANADA

HUDSON BAY

BAFFIN BAY

GREENLAND

LABRADOR SEA

GREENLAND SEA

NORTH ATLANTIC OCEAN

ICELAND

THE SNOWY OWL

Unusually for owls, the snowy owl hunts by day, locating prey by sight and sound. Their distinctive white plumage offers them the perfect camouflage against the snow.

SEASONAL WARDROBES

Many Arctic animals, like the arctic fox, have a summer and a winter coat so they remain camouflaged in snow or when the snow melts to reveal the ground beneath. The Arctic hare is completely white in winter, but for two black spots on the ends of its ears. These hares are known to 'flock' – this is where a group of up to 3,000 can move, run and change direction in perfect synchronicity!

ARCTIC FOX
Vulpes lagopus

ARCTIC HARE
Lepus arcticus

LONG IN THE TOOTH

This huge member of the seal family can reach sizes of up to 3.6 metres and weigh up to 2,000 kilograms. The walrus can dive into the depths, feeding on small invertebrates and molluscs on the sea floor.

THE ARCTIC TERN

ARCTIC TERN
Sterna paradisaea

The migratory Arctic tern makes by far the longest regular migration of any known animal! It travels a whopping 70,900 kilometres in a year.

WALRUS
Odobenus rosmarus

MUSK OX
Ovibos moschatus

STRONG SURVIVORS

Musk oxen are one of a very small group of animals known as megafauna which have survived the impact of human activity on the environment. When threatened, herds of musk oxen display clever defence behaviour, bunching together and brandishing their horns to form an impenetrable line.

NORTH AMERICA

Once a vast, sparsely populated wilderness, North America has witnessed the growth of one of the most powerful nations on Earth. In the process, nature has both suffered and benefited from human expansion, but there are many places in North America that are still wild.

LIFE CYCLE OF SALMON

When salmon return to the riverbed to spawn, they go through extreme physical changes: males grow a hump on their back, canines and a 'hook' on their mouth.

GRIZZLY BEAR
Ursus arctos

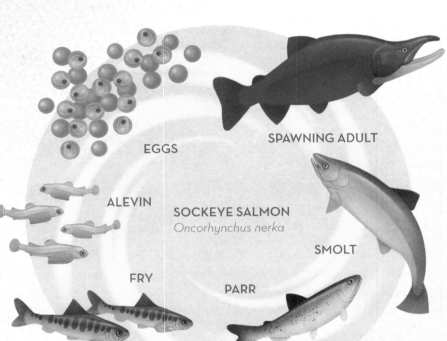

EGGS

SPAWNING ADULT

ALEVIN

SOCKEYE SALMON
Oncorhynchus nerka

SMOLT

FRY

PARR

FISH FOOD

Every summer, salmon return from the sea, swimming up streams and rivers against powerful currents. During this 'salmon run', large groups of grizzly bears gather at riverbanks and streams to hunt their quarry.

BROOKS RANGE

ALASKA RANGE

GULF OF ALASKA

THE GREY WOLF

Grey wolves are the largest member of the dog family (canidae) and are incredibly smart. Hunting in packs, they can take down prey up to ten times their size!

GREY WOLF
Canis lupus

THE PRAIRIE

The tall grass prairie is home to the bison, the elk and the prairie dog. Since European settlement and the introduction of modern agriculture, the prairie has shrunk to just two per cent of its former size. It is now considered an endangered habitat.

AMERICAN BISON
Bison bison

ELK
Cervus canadensis

GUNNISON'S PRAIRIE DOG
Cynomys gunnisoni

A NATIONAL EMBLEM

Named for the patch of white feathers on its head, the majestic bald eagle is the national symbol of the United States of America. Bald eagle pairs build their nests together, adding to them over many years.

BALD EAGLE
Haliaeetus leucocephalus

PACIFIC OCEAN

CASCADES

Snake

ROCKY MOUNTAINS

GREAT PLAINS

SIERRA NEVADA

COLUMBIA PLATEAU

Columbia

Colorado

COLUMBIA PLATEAU

Rio Grande

Missouri

Arkansas

EDWARDS PLATEAU

Ohio

Mississippi

APPALACHIANS

ATLANTIC OCEAN

COSTAL PLAIN

Gulf of Mexico

SEA OTTER
Enhydra lutris

ANIMAL ENGINEER

Beavers are nature's best engineers. Using their razor sharp teeth, they fell trees to make lodges, creating areas of calm, open water that can be easily protected from predators.

NORTH AMERICAN BEAVER
Castor canadensis

SEEING STARS

The star-nosed mole is named for the peculiar set of 22 tentacles that surround its nose. They use these tentacles to see (or rather, feel) where they're going!

STAR-NOSED MOLE
Condylura cristata

DIFFERENT DIETS

Raccoons have adapted well to living on the fringes of human settlements. With their unfussy eating and curious natures, they often rip open rubbish bags in search of food. Meanwhile, beautiful ivory-billed woodpeckers use their powerful beaks to make holes in trees and feast on the delicious beetle larvae within.

RACCOON
Procyon lotor

IVORY-BILLED WOODPECKER
Campephilus principalis

HAWAII

West of San Francisco lie the islands of Hawaii, which were created by underwater volcanic eruptions. It is the tops of those volcanoes that we now know as Hawaii.

HAWAIIAN HOARY BAT
Lasiurus semotus

EUPITHECIA MOTH LARVA
Eupithecia orichloris

PACIFIC OCEAN

NIIHAU

KAUAI

OAHU

MOLOKAI

LANAI

MAUI

KAHOOLAWE

HAWAII

PACIFIC GOLDEN PLOVER
Pluvialis fulva

DID YOU KNOW?

Over 95 per cent of all the insects on the islands aren't found anywhere else on Earth – and there are over ten thousand different species of them, including carnivorous caterpillars like the larva of the eupithecia moth! The Hawaiian hoary bat flies around the early night sky, snapping up moths and other invertebrates.

BIRDWATCHER'S HEAVEN

Hawaii is an amazing place to go birdwatching. You might see a Hawaiian stilt in the shallow waters, or a pacific golden plover which has flown all the way from the Arctic. The most incredible kinds of birds in Hawaii are the honey creepers, and the 'akiapōlā'au is one of the strangest – its beak is adapted for scraping away tree bark and probing around for tasty grubs.

'AKIAPŌLĀ'AU
Hemignathus munroi

HAWAIIAN STILT
Himantopus mexicanus knudseni

NENE
Branta sandvicensis

A NEW LAND

When Hawaii's islands were new, there were no native ground-living animals there. It was a paradise for animals that could fly to the islands, like birds and insects.
When animals are separated from others of their species, they can change in appearance over time. The beautiful nene is descended from a type of goose that settled on the islands many years ago and now looks very different from its Canadian relatives.

THE SOLENODON

SOLENODON
Solenodon paradoxus

Over to the east lie the Caribbean islands where odd animals like the solenodon survive as one of the only venomous mammals. It uses its long nose to push into the ground and smell out insects.

THE PAMPAS: PREDATORS AND PREY

Towards the south lies the Pampas, a cooler land where tall, tufty pampas grass grows. The pampas fox eats almost anything it can find, including armadillos. Armadillos protect themselves from the sharp teeth of foxes with their shield-like armour. The pink fairy armadillo burrows under the ground for an extra layer of protection.

PAMPAS FOX
Lycalopex gymnocercus

PINK FAIRY ARMADILLO
Chlamyphorus truncatus

NINE-BANDED ARMADILLO
Dasypus novemcinctus

DID YOU KNOW?

The nine-banded armadillo gives birth to one of the strangest families in the animal kingdom: not twins, or triplets, but always quadruplets, and all identical!

THE RHEA

One of the largest birds on Earth lives in the Pampas. Rheas have long wings that are useless for flying. But they do have long legs with powerful, clawed feet, which can carry them over 35 miles per hour to escape predators.

GREATER RHEA
Rhea americana

Map labels

Rio Orinoco
GUIANA HIGHLANDS
EQUATOR
Rio Negro
Amazon
AMAZON BASIN
Rio Madeira
Rio Xingu
BRAZILIAN HIGHLANDS
ANDES MOUNTAINS
MATO GROSSO PLATEAU
Rio Paraguai
Rio Sao Francisco
Titicaca Lake
NORTH ATLANTIC OCEAN
TROPIC OF CAPRICORN
ATACAMA DESERT
Pampas
SOUTH PACIFIC OCEAN
Strait of Magellan

THE ANDES

For five thousand miles, the Andes mountain chain reaches up along the west of South America, separating a sliver of coast from the centre of the continent.

THE HEIGHT OF COOL

Llamas and alpacas protect themselves against the cold with very dense wool. A bigger problem than the cold is the lack of oxygen as the higher you go, the less there is. The blood of these mammals has chemicals that allow more oxygen to be absorbed, so they can breathe easy. The closely-related vicuña has been recorded as living at 5,486 metres, high up in the Peruvian Andes!

ANDEAN CONDOR
Vultur gryphus

THE ANDEAN CONDOR

One of the largest wingspans of any living bird belongs to the Andean condor. Although they are heavy, they use very little energy when flying. This is because they mostly soar rather than flapping, using the air around them to carry them aloft updrafts.

TROPICAL ANDES

CENTRAL ANDES

AUSTRAL ANDES

ALPACA
Vicugna pacos

MOUNTAIN TAPIR
Tapirus pinchaque

LLAMA
Lama glama

AMONG THE CLOUDS

A little lower are the Andean cloud forests. Here you can find the spectacled bear, which hunts the mountain tapir. Like other tapirs, it has a small trunk on the front of its face, but to cope with the colder climate it is also covered in a woolly coat.

VICUÑA
Vicugna vicugna

OLINGUITO
Bassaricyon neblina

SPECTACLED BEAR
Tremarctos ornatus

DID YOU KNOW?

Many new species are being found in these cloud forests, like the olinguito – a solitary mammal related to raccoons. It was only discovered by zoologists in 2013!

GALÁPAGOS

Almost one thousand miles to the west of Ecuador are nineteen very special volcanic islands. A current of cold water means the temperature isn't desperately hot, and a fair amount of rain falls throughout the year.

GALÁPAGOS PENGUIN
Spheniscus mendiculus

Map labels:
Darwin
Wolf
PACIFIC OCEAN
Pinta
Marchena
Genovesa
EQUATOR
San Salvador
Baltra
Fernandina
Santa Cruz
Isabela
Santa Fe
San Cristóbal
Floreana
Española

UNIQUE SPECIES

Some animals could never survive the thousand-mile journey over the salty sea, which is why no frogs or toads are found on the islands. But once species did arrive, they began to change and specialise. Tortoises grew very large and now behave like grazing mammals. The cool waters also allow the Galápagos penguin to live comfortably around the islands, and it is not found anywhere else on Earth.

GALÁPAGOS TORTOISE
Chelonoidis nigra

Finch diagram labels:
WOODPECKER FINCH
Camarhynchus pallidus
LARGE GROUND FINCH
Geospiza magnirostris
GREEN WARBLER FINCH
Certhidea olivacea
VEGETARIAN FINCH
Platyspiza crassirostris
SHARP-BEAKED GROUND FINCH
Geospiza difficilis
GRUBS
SEEDS
INSECTS
FLOWERS LEAVES
EGGS BLOOD
ANCESTOR FINCH

DID YOU KNOW?

Scraping algae off marine rocks is very unusual for lizards, but marine iguanas evolved to do this after their ancestors arrived on the islands millions of years ago.

THE ORIGIN OF DARWIN'S THEORY

Charles Darwin spent five weeks on the islands in 1835. While there he realised that many of the animals from different islands (like finches) looked similar, but had slight differences. After years of thought, he discovered that all finches had the same ancestor. When separated on different islands, these finches had developed different beaks that suited their respective environment and diets. Thanks to his visit to the Galápagos Islands, Darwin had uncovered the secret of the origin of new species: evolution.

MARINE IGUANA
Amblyrhynchus cristatus

EUROPE

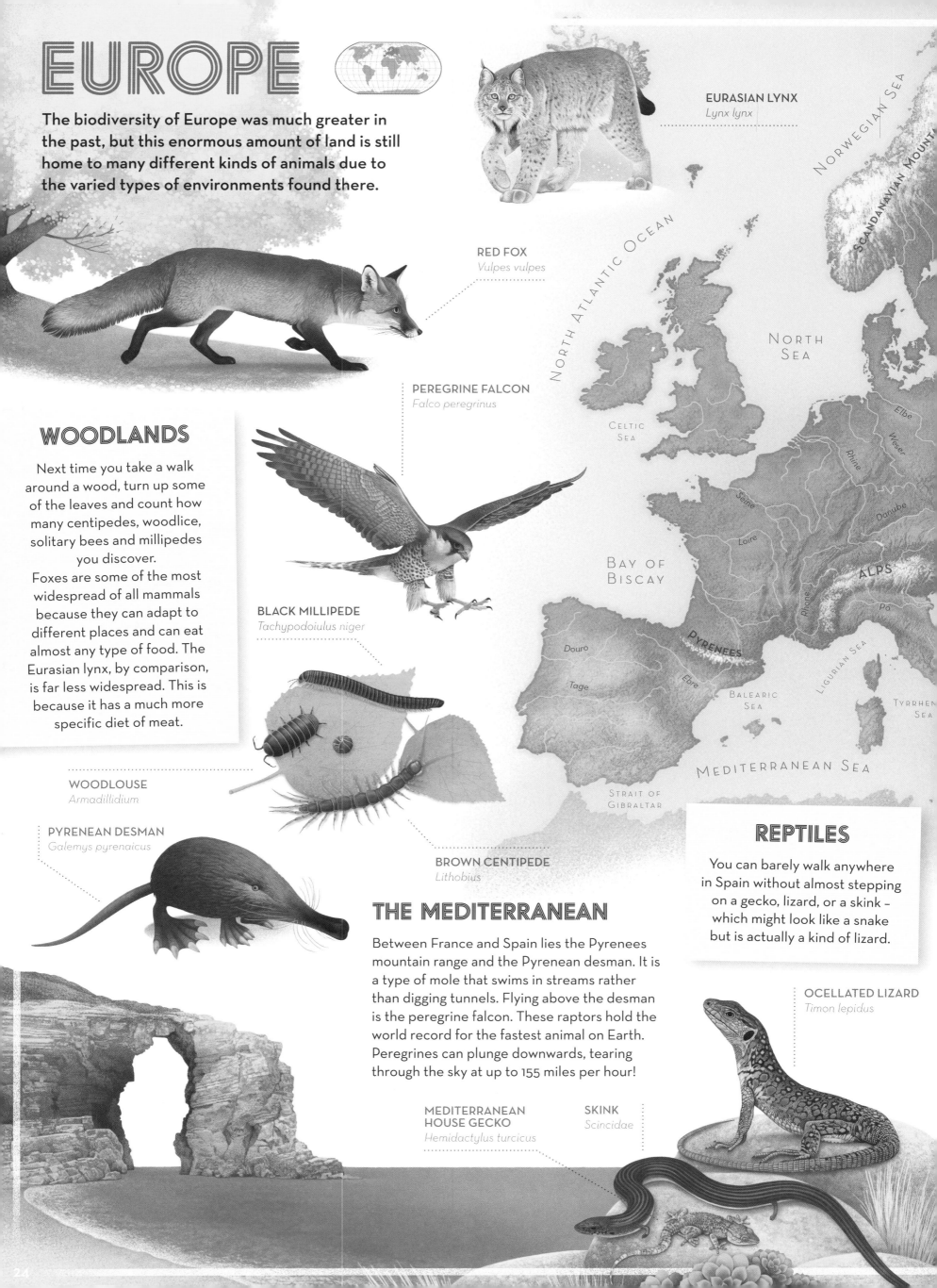

The biodiversity of Europe was much greater in the past, but this enormous amount of land is still home to many different kinds of animals due to the varied types of environments found there.

EURASIAN LYNX
Lynx lynx

RED FOX
Vulpes vulpes

PEREGRINE FALCON
Falco peregrinus

WOODLANDS

Next time you take a walk around a wood, turn up some of the leaves and count how many centipedes, woodlice, solitary bees and millipedes you discover.
Foxes are some of the most widespread of all mammals because they can adapt to different places and can eat almost any type of food. The Eurasian lynx, by comparison, is far less widespread. This is because it has a much more specific diet of meat.

BLACK MILLIPEDE
Tachypodoiulus niger

WOODLOUSE
Armadillidium

PYRENEAN DESMAN
Galemys pyrenaicus

BROWN CENTIPEDE
Lithobius

THE MEDITERRANEAN

Between France and Spain lies the Pyrenees mountain range and the Pyrenean desman. It is a type of mole that swims in streams rather than digging tunnels. Flying above the desman is the peregrine falcon. These raptors hold the world record for the fastest animal on Earth. Peregrines can plunge downwards, tearing through the sky at up to 155 miles per hour!

MEDITERRANEAN HOUSE GECKO
Hemidactylus turcicus

SKINK
Scincidae

REPTILES

You can barely walk anywhere in Spain without almost stepping on a gecko, lizard, or a skink – which might look like a snake but is actually a kind of lizard.

OCELLATED LIZARD
Timon lepidus

NORWEGIAN SEA

SCANDANAVIAN MOUNTAINS

NORTH ATLANTIC OCEAN

NORTH SEA

CELTIC SEA

Elbe

Weser

Rhine

Seine

Loire

Danube

BAY OF BISCAY

ALPS

Rhone

Po

PYRENEES

Douro

Ebre

LIGURIAN SEA

Tage

BALEARIC SEA

TYRRHENIAN SEA

MEDITERRANEAN SEA

STRAIT OF GIBRALTAR

NORTHERN CONIFER FORESTS

In the colder north of Europe are the conifer forests, where the trees have leaves all year round. Here you can find brown bears in the same territory as wild boar. A wander in Polish woodlands might bring you face to snout with the European bison.

WILD BOAR
Sus scrofa

BROWN BEAR
Ursus arctos

EUROPEAN BISON
Bison bonasus

DID YOU KNOW?

The huge comb-like structures on the front of the emperor moth's head are antennae! These moths have an amazing ability to detect chemicals in the air in the same way we use our noses to smell.

EMPEROR MOTH
Saturnia pavonia

INCREDIBLE CLIMBERS

Alpine ibex are easy to spot thanks to the males' enormous horns, but it is their ability to climb the steepest slopes in search of food that makes them superbly adapted for life in the Alps.

ALPINE MARMOT
Marmota marmota

ALPINE IBEX
Capra ibex

MARVELOUS MARMOTS

Higher than the Pyrenees is the Alps mountain range, where the chunky alpine marmot can be found. Having a larger body protects animals from the cold, as the larger you grow, the less heat you lose in relation to your body mass. Marmots are bigger members of the same mammal family as squirrels. They live in large colonies, munching on grass and relying on each other to squeak when danger is spotted.

URAL MOUNTAINS
Lake Onega
Lake Ladoga
BOTHNIA
BALTIC SEA
Volga
Vistula
CARPATHIAN MOUNTAINS
BLACK SEA
DINARIC ALPS
Danube
ADRIATIC SEA
IONIAN SEA
AEGEAN SEA

ASIA

The site of many of the world's first civilizations, Asia is Earth's largest and most populated continent. It has a mix of different climates across its many regions, from the hot desert in the middle east to Siberia – a wilderness of forests, tundra and taiga.

RACCOON DOG
Nyctereutes procyonoides

WILD DOGS AND BIG CATS

The raccoon dog is the only member of the dog family that is known to hibernate, but it is the big cats that are best adapted to the cold. The snow leopard has huge nasal cavities behind its nose to warm up the air, short legs that retain more body warmth, and very thick fur. The Siberian or Amur tiger is so successful at hunting that bears follow them to scavenge off their kills.

SNOW LEOPARD
Panthera uncia

AMUR TIGER
Panthera tigris altaica

SOLITARY SEALS

Lake Baikal is the world's deepest lake. It is covered in ice for most of the year and home to the Baikal seal. They began living here 400,000 years ago and are now one of the most isolated seal species on the planet.

BAIKAL SEAL
Pusa sibirica

SIBERIAN FLYING SQUIRREL
Pteromys volans

DID YOU KNOW?

The Siberian flying squirrel flies by stretching out the flaps of skin between its front and back legs (called the patagium). It can glide from one tree to another, without worrying about the raccoon dogs below.

Map labels: BARENTS SEA, BLACK SEA, CASPIAN SEA, ARAL SEA, URAL MOUNTAINS, Ob, Irtysh, Lake Balkhash, ZAGROS MOUNTAINS, TAKLA MAKAN DESERT, HIMALAYAS, Ganges, ARABIAN SEA, DECCAN PLATEAU, WESTERN GHATS, EASTERN GHATS, BAY OF BENGAL, LACCADIVE SEA

SOUTH EAST ASIA

South East Asia is a huge area that includes Indonesia, the Philippines, Papua New Guinea, Malaysia, Thailand and Vietnam to the north. Although huge amounts of land are being cleared by humans to grow crops like palm oil, South East Asia still remains a biodiversity hotspot.

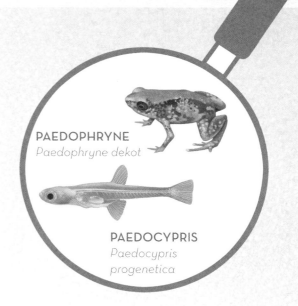

PAEDOPHRYNE
Paedophryne dekot

PAEDOCYPRIS
Paedocypris progenetica

MINIATURE WORLDS

Paedocypris is the smallest fish in the world and was found in the peat swamps of Sumatra, whilst the world's smallest frog, Paedophryne, lives in New Guinea. Both of these are less than 8 millimetres long, even when they are adults!

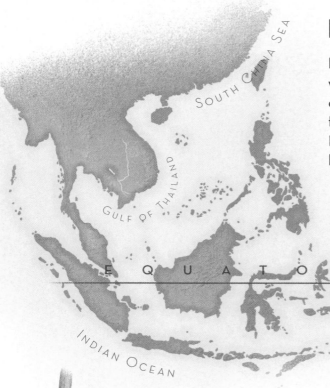

SOUTH CHINA SEA

GULF OF THAILAND

E Q U A T O R

INDIAN OCEAN

WALLACE'S FLYING FROG
Rhacophorus nigropalmatus

INSPIRING IDEAS OF EVOLUTION

The biologist Alfred Russell Wallace struck upon the idea of evolution when he was collecting and documenting the wildlife of Indonesia and Malaysia. One of the species that is named after him is Wallace's flying frog, which glides from tree to tree by stretching out the webs in-between its toes.

ELUSIVE MAMMALS

Swamps and cloud forests can get quite chilly, so it makes sense to have a thick coat like the Sumatran rhino. These rhinos are solitary creatures, and spotting them in the wild is extremely difficult. Orangutans are also hard to find, as they spend so much time up in the trees. They even sleep there, building a new nest every night from folded leaves.

BORNEAN ORANGUTAN
Pongo pygmaeus

SUMATRAN RHINO
Dicerorhinus sumatrensis

BEAUTIFUL FEATHERS

The six-plumed bird-of-paradise opens its feathers into a sort of tent and the king bird-of-paradise flutters its long red wings, whilst the blue bird-of-paradise hangs upside down, waving its brilliant plumage.

SIX-PLUMED BIRD-OF-PARADISE
Parotia lawesii

KING BIRD-OF-PARADISE
Cicinnurus regius

BLUE BIRD-OF-PARADISE
Paradisaea rudolphi

AFRICA

Five thousand miles from tip to tip, Africa is an enormous continent made up of 54 countries with a host of different environments. From vast deserts to steaming tropical rainforests, life flourishes in Africa, and it's where our own species first began its journey too.

EXPERT HERBIVORES

The giraffe's long neck allows it to reach six metres above the ground, using its long tongue to strip the leaves from branches, while the gerenuk can stand bolt upright to reach the highest leaves. Other herbivores like the scimitar oryx can survive without water for many weeks.

GIRAFFE
Giraffa

SCIMITAR ORYX
Oryx dammah

ATLANTIC OCEAN

ATLAS MOUNTAINS

TADEMAIT PLATEAU

Senegal

Niger

Volta

Lake Chad

GULF OF GUINEA

DID YOU KNOW?

The African bush elephant's huge ears cool their blood to stop them from overheating!

AFRICAN BUSH ELEPHANT
Loxodonta africana

LION
Panthera leo

BIG CATS

Most big cats rely on ambushing their prey, but the cheetah rockets after gazelle at about 62 miles per hour. The lion usually hunts at night and sleeps for about 21 hours a day. Lions live in family groups called prides that are made up of female relatives and their young, with one or more adult males.

CHEETAH
Acinonyx jubatus

THOMSON'S GAZELLE
Eudorcas thomsonii

RED-BILLED QUELEA
Quelea quelea

SHOEBILL
Balaeniceps rex

AFRICAN BIRDS

Billions of red-billed queleas are found throughout Sub-Saharan Africa. Other species, like the enormous shoebill, have grown very large and hunt lungfish, scooping them out of the mud with their huge beaks.

GERENUK
Litocranius walleri

RAINFORESTS

Extending out from the Congo river, the vast Congo rainforest reaches far north, nearly three thousand miles across the continent.

STRANGE STRENGTH

Some of the strangest creatures that live in the forests are the smallest, like the hero shrew. It has a reinforced backbone that is strong enough to withstand the weight of a fully grown person standing on it.

HIPPOPOTAMUS
Hippopotamus amphibius

HERO SHREW
Scutisorex somereni

PINK POWER

Within the Congo river swims the hippopotamus. These impressive creatures may seem hardy, but they still have to worry about the sun. When they are out of the water, they release a pink oil onto their skin which protects them from sunburn.

MOUNTAIN GORILLA
Gorilla beringei beringei

DID YOU KNOW?

A hippopotamus can weigh over four tonnes, and their front teeth can grow up to half a metre long!

SILVER LINING

Higher up, in the Virunga cloud forest, the mountain gorilla lives in large social groups. The backs of the male gorillas turn grey as they grow older, so they are known as 'silverbacks'.

Map labels: ANEAN SEA, Suez Canal, Nile, RED SEA, White Nile, Blue Nile, GREAT RIFT VALLEY, CONGO BASIN, Congo, Lake Albert, EQUATOR, INDIAN OCEAN, Lake Victoria, Lake Tanganyika, KATANGA PLATEAU, Lake Nyasa, Zambezi, MADAGASCAR, MOZAMBIQUE CHANNEL, range, DRAKENSBERG

DESERT

Even drier than the savannahs are the deserts, where the landscape is dominated by miles of rolling dunes. The Sahara is by far the world's greatest desert: the vast, sun-scorched area is about the size of the entire continent of Australia!

DROMEDARY CAMEL
Camelus dromedarius

HORNED VIPER
Cerastes cerastes

LIBYAN DESERT

S A H A R A

NUBIAN DESERT

NAMIB DESERT

KALAHARI DESERT

SURVIVING THE HEAT

Many animals that live here have adapted to very high temperatures. The dromedary camel's thick fur coat actually stops the sun's rays from penetrating its skin, while the highly venomous hairy thick-tailed scorpion hides from the sun in the undergrowth, in burrows and unguarded shoes.

HAIRY THICK-TAILED SCORPION
Parabuthus villosus

SAND SWIMMING

Some mammals actually live within the sand. The giant golden mole swims through the sand, pushing itself with its powerful forelimbs. The horned viper is nicknamed the 'side-winder' because it moves along the dunes sideways leaving strange j-shaped markings in the sand.

MARTIAL EAGLE
Polemaetus bellicosus

THE MEERKAT

The Kalahari is known to many for its famous residents, the meerkats. To escape the hot sun, they live in burrows. They take it in turns to stand guard, scanning the horizon for predators like martial eagles.

GIANT GOLDEN MOLE
Chrysospalax trevelyani

MEERKAT
Suricata suricatta

MADAGASCAR

Madagascar has been separated from all other land for the last 88 million years, meaning that unique animals and plants evolved there in isolation. Although it is quite dry, a long strip of humid forest runs along the eastern coast.

MADAGASCAN PYGMY KINGFISHER
Corythornis madagascariensis

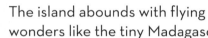

THE FOSSA

At six feet long, the fossa is Madagascar's largest predator. It looks like a large mongoose and preys on most Madagascan animals, including many unique species of lemur.

GIRAFFE WEEVIL
Trachelophorus giraffa

FOSSA
Cryptoprocta ferox

BLUE COUA
Coua caerulea

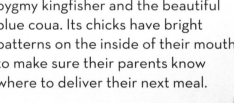

WEEVIL WORLD

Weevils are a very diverse type of beetle, and one of the most striking is found on this island. Although only two centimetres long, the giraffe weevil lives up to its name. They are hunted by stealthy sharp-shooters – the panther chameleon. It balances on branches using its clawed feet and focuses on its prey with independently moving eyes before ensnaring them with its long tongue.

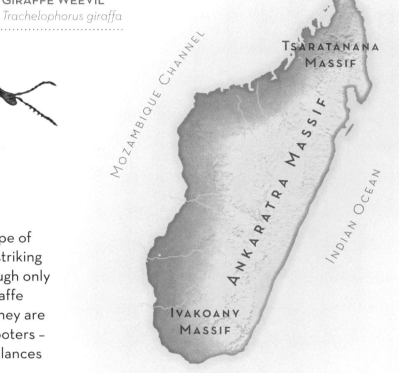

MOZAMBIQUE CHANNEL

TSARATANANA MASSIF

ANKARATRA MASSIF

INDIAN OCEAN

IVAKOANY MASSIF

BIRD HEAVEN

The island abounds with flying wonders like the tiny Madagascan pygmy kingfisher and the beautiful blue coua. Its chicks have bright patterns on the inside of their mouths to make sure their parents know where to deliver their next meal.

COQUEREL'S SIFAKA
Propithecus coquereli

DID YOU KNOW?

Living here is the world's smallest chameleon, Brookesia micra, which is less then two centimetres long.

LEAF CHAMELEON
Brookesia micra

RING-TAILED LEMUR
Lemur catta

PANTHER CHAMELEON
Furcifer pardalis

SMELLY LEMURS

Lemurs are unique to the island and display a range of behaviours. The ring-tailed lemur marks its territory with scent glands on its body, which tell other lemurs to keep out. The male ring-tail also uses his scent in "stink fights" with other males!

OCEANIA

The Pacific Ocean is an enormous swathe of sea, larger than all of the Earth's continents put together! Within this region of Oceania are twenty thousand tiny islands; home to an incredible abundance of life, as animals managed to find their way to these isolated lands and evolve.

GIANTS OF OCEANIA

The massive coconut crab can weigh over four kilograms and the giant clam is one of the largest molluscs, growing to more than a metre across. Gliding through the water above is the green sea turtle – one of the most majestic animals in the Pacific. This docile vegetarian only breaks the surface of the ocean to breathe. Females haul themselves on land to lay eggs in the sand, away from marine predators.

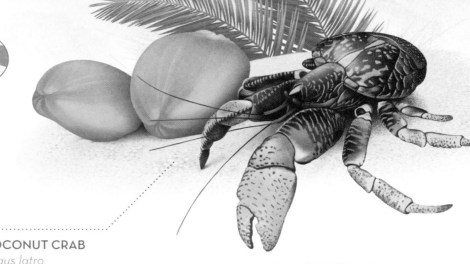

COCONUT CRAB
Birgus latro

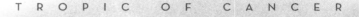

TROPIC OF CANCER

NORTHERN
MARIANA ISLANDS

MARSHALL
ISLANDS

PHILIPPINE
SEA

CAROLINE ISLANDS

KIRIBA

SOLOMON
ISLANDS

TUVALU

GREAT BARRIER REEF

CORAL
SEA

NEW
CALEDONIA

VANUATU

FIJI

GREEN SEA TURTLE
Chelonia mydas

DEADLY SEA CREATURES

Box jellyfish and sea snakes are extremely venomous – the olive sea snake is one of the most dangerous snakes in the world.

BOX JELLYFISH
Chironex fleckeri

RADIANT REEFS

Coral reefs live in symbiosis with algae; in return for sharing food with the corals, algae are allowed to shelter inside the reef. The reefs are also home to the coloured Christmas tree worms and nudibranchs – a type of soft mollusc.

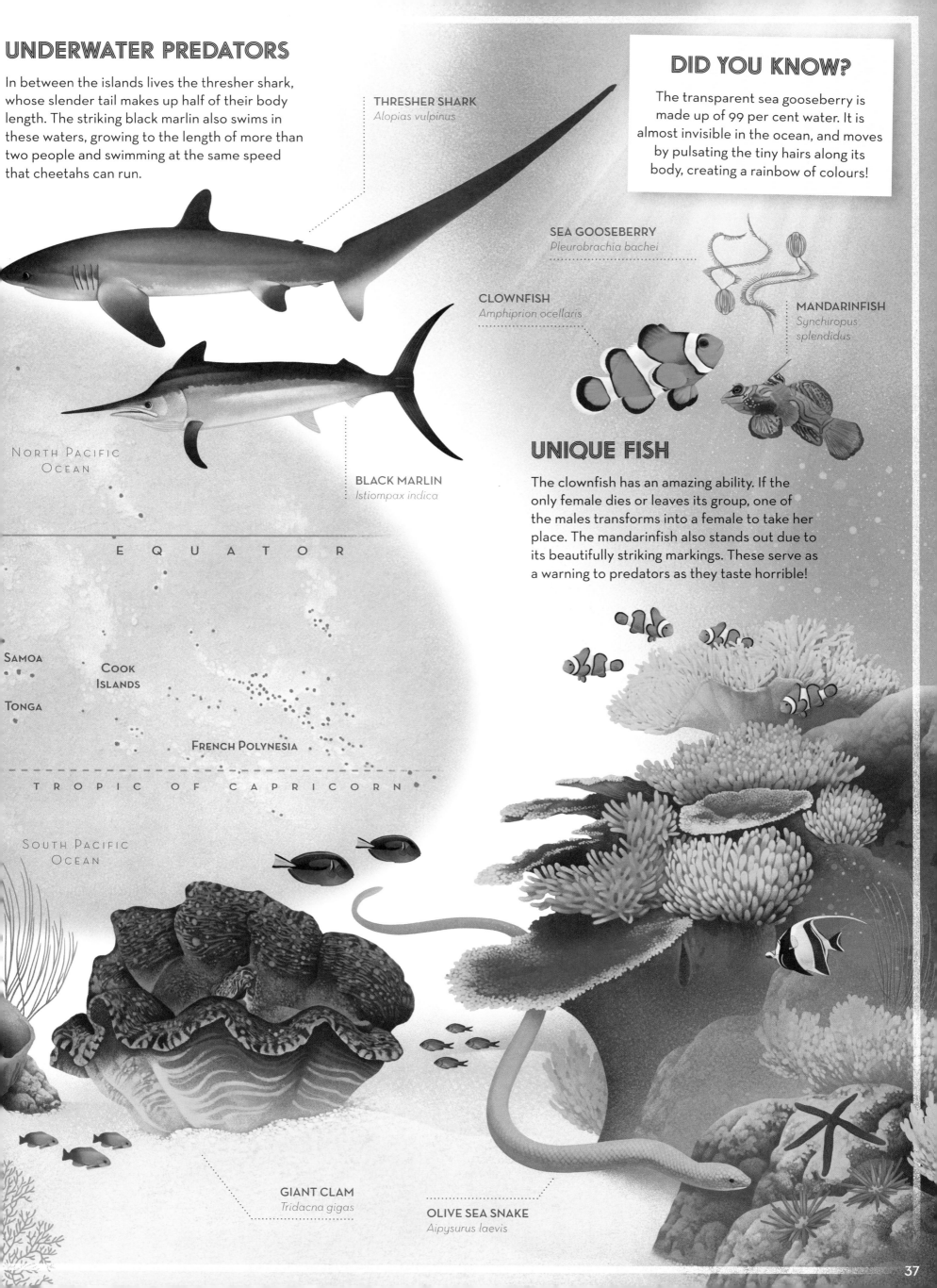

UNDERWATER PREDATORS

In between the islands lives the thresher shark, whose slender tail makes up half of their body length. The striking black marlin also swims in these waters, growing to the length of more than two people and swimming at the same speed that cheetahs can run.

THRESHER SHARK
Alopias vulpinus

DID YOU KNOW?

The transparent sea gooseberry is made up of 99 per cent water. It is almost invisible in the ocean, and moves by pulsating the tiny hairs along its body, creating a rainbow of colours!

SEA GOOSEBERRY
Pleurobrachia bachei

CLOWNFISH
Amphiprion ocellaris

MANDARINFISH
Synchiropus splendidus

NORTH PACIFIC OCEAN

BLACK MARLIN
Istiompax indica

E Q U A T O R

UNIQUE FISH

The clownfish has an amazing ability. If the only female dies or leaves its group, one of the males transforms into a female to take her place. The mandarinfish also stands out due to its beautifully striking markings. These serve as a warning to predators as they taste horrible!

SAMOA

COOK ISLANDS

TONGA

FRENCH POLYNESIA

T R O P I C   O F   C A P R I C O R N

SOUTH PACIFIC OCEAN

GIANT CLAM
Tridacna gigas

OLIVE SEA SNAKE
Aipysurus laevis

AUSTRALASIA

Lying between the Indian and Pacific Ocean is three million square miles of zoological excitement: Australia. It is the flattest continent and one of the driest.

THE OUTBACK

Most animals couldn't survive in the arid Outback, but a few thrive. The thorny devil is covered in spines that protect it from becoming someone else's lunch, and it has tiny channels in between its scales that guide any rain water straight into its mouth. Also roaming the ground is the golden bowerbird, named after the impressive and beautiful structures it creates out of twigs, sticks and stones to attract a mate.

GOLDEN BOWERBIRD
Prionodura newtoniana

INDIAN OCEAN

GULF OF CARPENTARIA

KING LEOPOLD RANGE

MacDONNELL RANGES

A U S T R A L I A

SIMPSON DESERT

GREAT VICTORIA DESERT

LAKE EYRE

DARLING RANGE

GREAT AUSTRALIAN BIGHT

THORNY DEVIL
Moloch horridus

PLATYPUS
Ornithorhynchus anatinus

DID YOU KNOW?

The platypus has a duck-bill, which is an electroreception device. It can sense the movement of prey even with its eyes (and ears) closed.

RAINFORESTS AND WOODS OF NORTH AUSTRALIA

Much of Australia is covered in desert, but large areas are blanketed in rainforests. It is here that the platypus lives, eating crustaceans under the surface of fresh water.

IN THE TREES

The blue-winged kookaburra swoops down to feed on animals that live close to the ground, from insects to small mammals. Meanwhile, the koala lives in the dense woods. The koala's hands are the most interesting – its first finger juts out like another thumb, making holding onto branches much easier.

BLUE-WINGED KOOKABURRA
Dacelo leachii

KOALA
Phascolarctos cinereus

NEW ZEALAND

A thousand miles off the coast of Australia is the temperate island of New Zealand. It has been isolated for thousands of years and has developed a very distinct range of animal life.

GREAT BARRIER REEF

GREAT DIVIDING RANGE

BASS STRAIT

TASMANIA

TASMAN SEA

NEW ZEALAND

FLIGHTLESS BIRDS

Due to a lack of predators, many of New Zealand's birds evolved to become flightless, such as the kiwi and the kakapo – and there are only about one hundred kakapos left. The giant moa became extinct long ago, having been hunted by the first humans that arrived on the island.

GIANT MOA
Dinornis

KAKAPO
Strigops habroptilus

DID YOU KNOW?

The huge perentie shakes its prey to death using nothing but its jaws. It is one of the only lizards that can sprint after its prey for a long time, so good luck running away from it!

NORTH ISLAND BROWN KIWI
Apteryx mantelli

TASMANIA

The island of Tasmania is home to spectacular mountains and national parks. It is a much wetter place than Australia, and far cooler too. During the night, the Tasmanian devil stalks the forest floor, its long whiskers twitching to find its way.

PERENTIE
Varanus giganteus

COMMON WOMBAT
Vombatus ursinus

TASMANIAN DEVIL
Sarcophilus harrisii

MARVELOUS MARSUPIALS

Most species of marsupial (a type of mammal) live in Australasia, and many keep their young in pouches. Wallabies and kangaroos are widespread here, bounding across the plains using both of their legs at the same time. Wombats dig large tunnel systems and spend much of their time underground, where they eat a vegetarian diet.

RED KANGAROO
Macropus rufus

YELLOW-FOOTED ROCK-WALLABY
Petrogale xanthopus

ANTARCTICA

The Earth's southernmost and coldest continent, Antarctica is surrounded by the icy Southern Ocean, and contains the world's geographic and magnetic South Poles. It is covered in the single largest mass of ice on Earth! In the summer months (December-February), its coastal regions and seas are teeming with life, as millions of penguins, seals, cetaceans and sea birds come to feed and breed.

DID YOU KNOW?

During springtime over 100 million birds come to Antarctica to breed, including the blue-eyed cormorant and the snow petrel.

SNOW PETREL
Pagodroma nivea

BLUE-EYED CORMORANT
Phalacrocorax atriceps

ELEPHANT SEAL
Mirounga leonina

SPECTACULAR SEALS

The large-jawed, sharp-toothed leopard seal is actually in the same family as the harmless looking fur and Weddell seals. It can grow up to three and a half metres in length and feeds on penguins, fish and even other seals! Elephant seals can hold their breath for up to 100 minutes – longer than any non-cetacean (non-whale like) mammal.

WEDDELL SEAL
Leptonychotes weddellii

FUR SEAL
Arctocephalus gazella

LEOPARD SEAL
Hydrurga leptonyx

ADÉLIE PENGUIN
Pygoscelis adeliae

ANTARCTIC CIRCLE

WEDDELL SEA

RONNE ICE SHELF

SOUTH POLE

MARIE BYRD LAND

AMUNDSEN SEA

ROSS ICE SHELF

ROSS SEA

THE EMPEROR PENGUIN

The emperor penguins are the largest penguins and there are over 17 species living here! They are the only animal to permanently live on Antarctica and breed during its unforgiving winter. The female emperor penguin hatches a single egg that must be carefully passed to the males without allowing it to touch the freezing ground. The males take care of the eggs by balancing them on their feet.

NATURE'S GIANTS

The largest known animal to have ever lived is the mighty blue whale, which can grow to 30 metres in length. This whale and the humpback whale feed on millions of tiny crustaceans called krill, unlike the orca which eats marine mammals and birds. The colossal squid is the largest known invertebrate alive today, reaching up to 14 metres in length – the size of an average bus!

ANTARCTIC KRILL
Euphausia superba

BLUE WHALE - 30 metres
Balaenoptera musculus

HUMPBACK WHALE - 16 metres
Megaptera novaeangliae

QUEEN MAUD
LAND

EAST ANTARCTIC
ICE SHEET

EMPEROR PENGUIN
Aptenodytes forsteri

WILKES LAND

COLOSSAL SQUID - 14 metres
Mesonychoteuthis hamiltoni

SOUTHERN OCEAN

VICTORIA
LAND

ORCA - 8 metres
Orcinus orca

UNDER THE ICE

The freezing Southern Ocean is perfect for unusual creatures like the crocodile icefish, starfish and the newly discovered Antarctic sea anemone that resides in burrows dug into the bottom of the sea ice.

MACARONI PENGUIN
Eudyptes chrysolophus

SEA ANEMONE
Urticinopsis antarctica

STARFISH
Odontaster validus

CROCODILE ICEFISH
Chionodraco hamatus

ANIMALS IN CRISIS

We have met many animals in this Animal Atlas but, sadly, many species are at risk of going extinct which means disappearing forever. Species naturally go extinct (we know that from studying fossils), but the rate that species are becoming endangered is now very high.

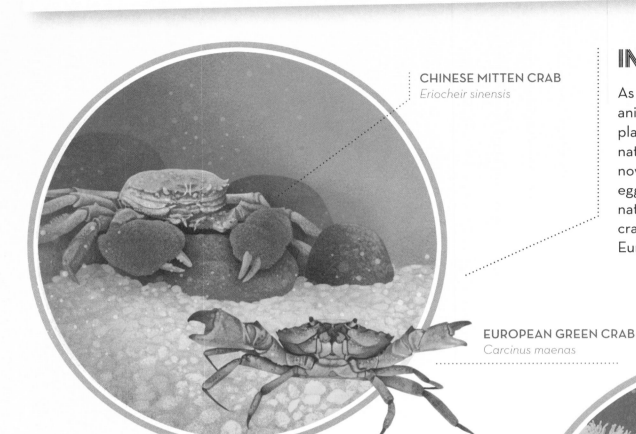

CHINESE MITTEN CRAB
Eriocheir sinensis

EUROPEAN GREEN CRAB
Carcinus maenas

INTRODUCED SPECIES

As humans have moved around the world, other animals have travelled with them. On reaching new places, these animals can have terrible impacts on native ecosystems. Many sea birds in the Pacific are now endangered because introduced rats eat their eggs. Some introduced species also eat the food native animals need to survive – Chinese mitten crabs have become a problem for the survival of European green crabs.

ANTHIAS FISH
Anthias anthias

CLIMATE CHANGE

Due to negative human impact on the Earth, parts of the world are getting hotter, whilst other parts are getting wetter. If animals can't migrate to areas that suit their ideal temperature, they can't survive. Coral reefs are very sensitive to changing temperatures and die off when it gets too hot.

BORNEAN ORANGUTAN
Pongo pygmaeus

SUMATRAN RHINO
Dicerorhinus sumatrensis

BLUE-CHEEKED BUTTERFLYFISH
Chaetodon semilarvatus

HABITAT LOSS

Every day there are more and more humans, but this is bad news for animals. South East Asia's Sumatran rhino and orangutan are both being threatened with extinction as more forests are cut down to make way for human-grown crops such as palm oil, sugar cane and soya. As habitats are fragmented, it becomes difficult for animals to find each other and have offspring.

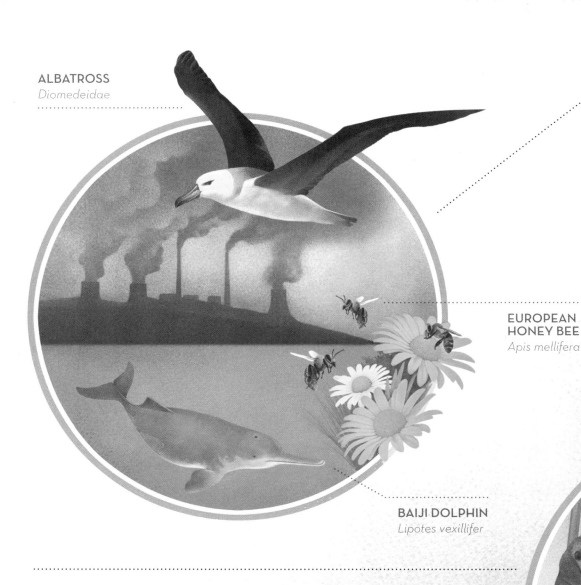

ALBATROSS
Diomedeidae

POLLUTION

Humans make a lot of mess. There are now vast amounts of plastic in the ocean (and in the stomachs of animals like albatrosses). Some of the worst pollution is seen in places like the Yangtze River, where the baiji dolphin is thought to have recently gone extinct. Many of the pesticides we use in farming are also a deadly threat to bees.

EUROPEAN
HONEY BEE
Apis mellifera

PANGOLIN
Pholidota

BAIJI DOLPHIN
Lipotes vexillifer

HUNTING

Large mammals such as the rhinoceros are hunted illegally, and parts of them – like their horns – are cut off and kept as trophies. Others like the pygmy slow loris are killed and used in traditional 'medicines' – even though these are completely useless. Animals such as pangolins are hunted in huge numbers to be eaten, and overfishing is having a huge effect on the wildlife of the oceans.

PYGMY SLOW LORIS
Nycticebus pygmaeus

A HELPING HAND

The International Union for the Conservation of Nature (IUCN) brings together experts to try to save endangered animals. It also keeps track of which animals need help in its 'Red List'.
The Convention on International Trade in Endangered Species (CITES) aims to stop people killing animals for trophies or keeping rare species as pets. Many international organisations such as the Zoological Society of London (ZSL) and the World Wildlife Fund (WWF) raise money to support vital conservation projects around the world.

DEFENDING OUR WORLD

Although some animals are fighting against extinction, there is good news. Many of the almost nine billion members of our species are helping day and night to make sure that they survive.

KEEP ON CONSERVING

The beautiful Mauritius kestrel lives on the same island as the dodo did, but thanks to a few dedicated people it won't suffer the same fate. Scientists realized it was rapidly declining in numbers due to human interference, so they set up efforts to save it. In 1974 there were only four of these birds in the world, but now there are more than 400.

BLUE-CAPPED MOTMOT
Momotus coeruliceps

ELEPHANT SEAL
Mirounga leonina

THE BIG PICTURE

For animals to survive, the environment around them needs to flourish as well. The Península Valdés Biosphere Reserve in Argentina is over four million acres of protected land – a haven free from human disruption for elephant seals, Magellanic penguins, and southern right whales. In Ecuador, the Reserva Ecológica Comunal Loma Alta is a protected cloud forest where the blue-capped motmot thrives undisturbed by humans.

MAGELLANIC PENGUIN
Spheniscus magellanicus

SUSTAINABLE ENERGY

Most of the energy we use comes from fossil fuels: oil, coal, and gas. They are 'non-renewable', meaning that when they're gone, they're gone! They also release large amounts of carbon dioxide into the air when burned, which is changing the world's climate and affecting all living creatures. One alternative is solar energy. It doesn't come from the earth, it doesn't pump carbon dioxide into the air, and it's renewable! Our lovely sun is going to be around for another five billion years.

MAURITIUS KESTREL
Falco punctatus

WE'RE ALL IN THIS TOGETHER

One small way we can help is to buy paper from renewable sources as it ensures entire woodlands don't disappear. You've already started: the paper in this book has been certified by the Forest Stewardship Council.

But learning about animals is equally important. The more that we understand, enjoy and respect all species, the more we will be willing to make sure all living creatures have their fair share of our planet!

SOUTHERN RIGHT WHALE
Eubalaena australis

INDEX OF ANIMALS

FOR NIGEL COLLINS
– NC

FOR MY SON ELIA
– GB

Acknowledgements:

Nick Crumpton would like to thank Dr Matt Wilkinson,
Dr Rick Thompson, and the staff of the Natural
History Museum's London Library and Archives.

Alex Spiro would like to personally thank Gaia
and Nick and the entire team at Flying Eye Books,
especially Camille, Harriet, Hanna and Sam.

The Amazing Animal Atlas © Flying Eye Books 2017.

This is a first edition published in 2017 by Flying Eye Books,
an imprint of Nobrow Ltd. 27 Westgate Street, London E8 3RL.

Project conceived by Alex Spiro.
Text by Dr Nick Crumpton.
Illustrations by Gaia Bordicchia.
Edited by Harriet Birkinshaw and Hanna Milner.
Designed by Camille Pichon.

Published in the US by Nobrow (US) Inc.
Printed in Latvia on FSC® certified paper.
ISBN: 978-1-909263-11-6

Order from www.flyingeyebooks.com

REFERENCES AND EXTRA READING:

Balmford, A. (2012)

Wild Hope: On the Front Lines of Conservation Success, University of Chicago Press

Carwardine, M. (2013)

Natural History Museum Animal Records, Firefly Books

MacDonald, D.W. [ed] (2006)

The Encyclopedia of Mammals, Oxford University Press

Mulligan, M. (2015)

An introduction to sustainability: Environmental, social and personal perspectives, Routledge

Piper, R. (2015)

Animal Earth: The Amazing Diversity of Living Creatures, Thames and Hudson

Pullin, A.S. (2002)

Conservation Biology, Cambridge University Press

Wilson, E.O. (2001)

The Diversity of Life, Penguin

www.arkive.org

www.iucnredlist.org